Ten Little Fingers and Ten Little Toes

For Helena, who teaches them all
—M.F.—

For all the babies of the world
—H.O.—

First published 2008 by Walker Books Ltd
87 Vauxhall Walk, London SE11 5HJ

This edition published 2009

2 4 6 8 10 9 7 5 3 1

Text © 2008 Mem Fox
Illustrations © 2008 Helen Oxenbury

The right of Mem Fox and Helen Oxenbury to be identified as author and illustrator respectively of this work
has been asserted by them in accordance with the Copyright, Designs and Patents Act 1988

This book has been typeset in Giovanni Light.

Printed in China.

British Library Cataloguing in Publication Data: a catalogue record for this book is available from the British Library

ISBN 978-1-4063-1956-9

www.walker.co.uk

Ten Little Fingers and Ten Little Toes

Written by *Mem Fox*   Illustrated by *Helen Oxenbury*

WALKER BOOKS
AND SUBSIDIARIES

LONDON • BOSTON • SYDNEY • AUCKLAND

There was one little baby who was born far away.

And another who was born on the very next day.

And both of these babies,

as everyone knows,

had ten little fingers

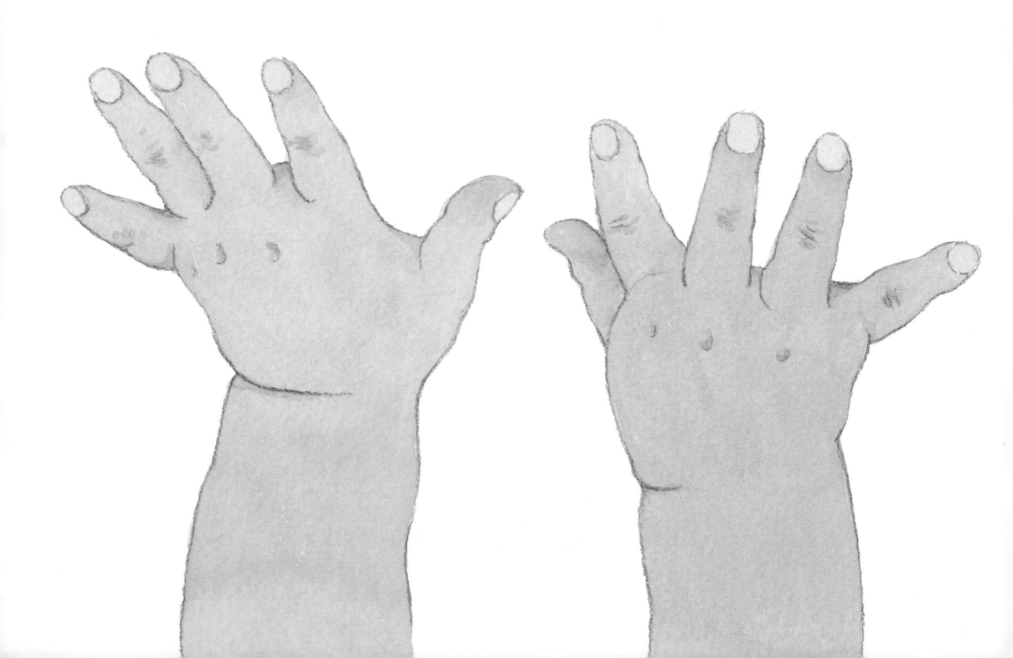

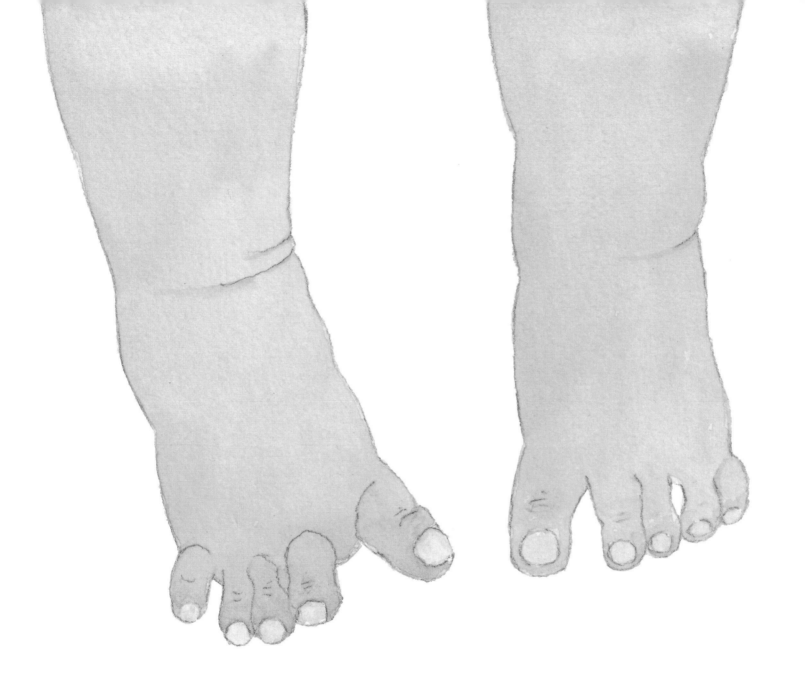

and ten little toes.

There was one little baby who was born in a town.

And another who was wrapped in an eiderdown.

And both of these babies,

as everyone knows,

had ten little fingers

and ten little toes.

There was one little baby who was born in the hills.

And another who suffered from sneezes and chills.

And both of these babies,

as everyone knows,

had ten little fingers

and ten little toes.

There was one little baby who was born on the ice.

And another in a tent, who was just as nice.

And both of these babies,

as everyone knows,

had ten little fingers

and ten little toes.

But the next baby born was truly divine,
a sweet little child who was mine, all mine.

And this little baby,

as everyone knows,

has ten little fingers,

ten little toes,

and three little kisses

on the tip of its nose.